The Challenge to Heal Workbook & Journal

The Challenge to Heal Workbook & Journal

Work Out & Release Trauma Resulting from High-Control Situations

Bonnie Zieman

Copyright © 2016 Bonnie Zieman
All rights reserved.

ISBN: 1539518930
ISBN 13: 9781539518938

"Writing is not only a reflection of what one thinks and feels but a rope one weaves with words that can lower you below or hoist you above the surface of your life, enabling you to go deeper or higher than you would otherwise go. What excites me about this metaphor is that it makes writing much more than a lifesaving venture."

Phyllis Theroux
The Journal Keeper: A Memoir

Contents

PART 1 Guidelines for Documenting Your High-Control Group Story · 1

- Document your history in the high-control group. · 5
- What was your daily/weekly life like as a member of a high-control group? · · · · · · · · · · · · · · · · · · · 7
- Document some of your specific experiences and relationships in the high-control group – ones that were rewarding, and ones that disturbed you. · 9
- What controls and pressures did you experience? ·12
- What thoughts, feelings, needs, desires, longings, impulses or actions did you have to suppress to survive in the controlling group? ·15
- Are there things that happened in the high-control milieu that you never told anyone and you want to record here? ·17
- Describe the thoughts and/or incidents that caused you to question and doubt the high-control group and your involvement with it: · 20
- How did you handle the doubts and cope with the questions about whether you might be in a destructive group? What did you feel at that time? · 23
- What resources or information helped you to begin to think about leaving, or did you have to figure it all out on your own? Explain. · 25
- What concerns or fears did you have about leaving? How did they affect your ability to leave? How did you overcome them? · 27
- How did your actual leaving of the high-control group unfold? ·31
- What were your experiences and feelings once you left? · 35
- Did you find yourself in a grieving process? How did you express your grief? · · · · · · · · · · · · · · · · · · 38
- Where do you stand now in relationship to the group that exploited you? How do you feel about that? · · ·41
- What hurts, indignities, wounds are still needing to be addressed? How are you dealing with them now? · 43
- How do you take care of yourself? How do you calm or soothe yourself? Are there things you have been intending to do to help yourself, but have not done yet? ·47
- Have you used psychotherapy to help deal with your wounds? How did it help? What did you learn? · · · · · 49
- If you have not been able to use therapy, what are your concerns about it? (Please revisit Chapter 28 in The Challenge to Heal book, page 200) ·51
- Are you aware of your current wants and needs? Describe them. · 52
- Have you noticed a shift in your values since leaving? Explain. · 54

Why People Join and Stay in High-Control Groups (The Challenge to Heal, Chapter 6, page 25) · · · · 56
Why do you think you joined or stayed in your high-control group or relationship? · 56
How will you attend to the particular need or inclination that pulled you into a destructive group or relationship, so that you do not become vulnerable to any further manipulation and exploitation? · · · · · · · · 57

What is to Be Gained by Leaving? (The Challenge to Heal, Chapter 7, page 38) · · · · · · · · · · · · · · · · · · 59
What specifically have you gained by exiting the high-control group or relationship? · · · · · · · · · · · · · · · · · · 59
Conversely, what challenges have you had to face because of leaving a high-control group? · · · · · · · · · · · · · 61

Stages of Change (The Challenge to Heal, Chapter 10, page 50) · 63
What stage do you think you are in in your transition? Describe it? · 63
Based on Chapter 10 in *The Challenge to Heal Book*, what do you need to do to move into the next stage of change? · 64

The Challenge of Becoming Comfortable with Feelings (The Challenge to Heal, Chapter 12, page 61) · · · · 65
How comfortable are you in dealing with difficult feelings? What feelings have been most present for you since leaving the high-control group? · 65

A Closer Look at the Most Challenging Feelings (The Challenge to Heal, Chapter 13, page 66) · · · · · · 67
Which of the feelings addressed in Chapter 13 of the book is most challenging for you, and why? · · · · · · · · · 67
What can you do about these challenging feelings (based on what you read in The Challenge to Heal, pages 66-81)? · 70

Challenge Thoughts of Suicide (The Challenge to Heal, Chapter 14, page 82) · 72
Have the aftereffects of leaving a high-control group ever caused you to contemplate ending your life? Describe. · 72
What are your current thoughts about suicide (after reading Chapter 14, pages 82-86 in The Challenge to Heal?) · 73

Dis-identify From Negative Beliefs, Thoughts, Feelings (The Challenge to Heal, Chapter 15, page 87) · · · · 76
What are the beliefs/thoughts/feelings that are most troubling for you now? · 76
How are you doing with the dis-identification technique, page 89? (It's a powerful tool and one that will serve you well throughout your life - once you incorporate it into your repertoire of healing skills.) · · · · · · · · 78

Emotions Manifesting As Physical Ailments (The Challenge to Heal, Chapter 16, page 93) · · · · · · · · · · · · 80
What has been your experience with physical ailments, possibly due to being in a high-control group? · · · · 80

Accepting Life As It Unfolds (The Challenge to Heal, Chapter 17, page 99) · 83
How often do you find yourself fighting against or resisting the flow of life or "what is"? · · · · · · · · · · · · · · · · 83

Do you still view yourself as a victim of the high-control group or relationship due to the controls and coercion? · 84
What can you do to move from victim to hero of your own story? (See pages 101-104, The Challenge to Heal) · · · 84

Who Are You Now, Without the Controls? (The Challenge to Heal, Chapter 18, page 105) 87
Did you have to build a false self to survive in the group? Explain. 87
How are you doing now in reclaiming your authentic identity? 89

The Challenge of Guilt (The Challenge to Heal, Chapter 19, page 111) 91
Have you been able to determine if you are carrying any shame or guilt due to the controls and coercion?
Based on what you read in Chapter 19, what kind of guilt are you dealing with? 91
What are your feelings about what you learned about "existential guilt"? 92

Tips for Healing from Negative Effects of High-Control Groups (The Challenge to Heal, Chapter 20, page 118) 94
Which tips from The Challenge to Heal, pages 118-154 have been most helpful for you? 94
Which tips do you still need to incorporate into your repertoire of healing tools? What is difficult about this for you? 96

Psychosocial Development Impeded By Imposed Controls (The Challenge to Heal, Chapter 21, page 157) ... 98
How might your normal development into a mature, capable adult have been interrupted by being in a high-control group (The Challenge to Heal, pages 157-165)? 98
What stages of development do you most need to address and incorporate now (trust, autonomy, initiative, industry, authentic identity, intimacy, caring, wisdom)? 99

Ultimate Concerns of Facing Life Free (The Challenge to Heal, Chapter 22, page 166) 102
How did you feel after reading the chapter on the existential givens (life's ultimate concerns) in The Challenge to Heal? 102
How might you have used membership in a high-control group to avoid the basic givens (aloneness, mortality, freedom/responsibility, meaning) of any human life? 103
How will you help yourself to confront these ultimate concerns of life now? 103

Self-Love & Self-Acceptance – Essential to Healing (The Challenge to Heal, Chapter 23, page 174) 104
How are you doing in the areas of self-acceptance and self-love now? 104
Are you using the **E**motional **F**reedom **T**echnique acupressure rubbing technique described in Chapter 23 of *The Challenge to Heal*? 107
How have you adapted the EFT statement (used while you rub the tender spot on your chest) to fit *your* needs? 107

Self-Acceptance Awakens a Sense of Belonging (The Challenge to Heal, Chapter 24, page 183) 109
How are you doing with creating a sense of belonging in your own heart? 109

Creative Visualization – A Healing Resource (The Challenge to Heal, Chapter 25, page 186) 111
Have you used guided meditations to help with your healing? How have you adapted meditations for your particular circumstances? 111

Acting As If (The Challenge to Heal, Chapter 26, page 192) · · · · · · 113
What do you think about "acting as if" as a technique to help with your recovery from undue controls? How have you employed it? · · · · · · 113

Embracing Other Movements, Groups or Religions (The Challenge to Heal, Chapter 27, page 197) · · · · · 115
What were your thoughts/reactions when you read this chapter about taking some time before joining other movements or groups? · · · · · · 115
Where do you stand with regard to gurus, causes, leaders, movements, god, religion, etc.? · · · · · · 116

The Challenge of Ostracism (The Challenge to Heal, Chapter 29, page 211) · · · · · · 117
Have you been cut off, alienated, shunned or disconnected from or by family and friends due to leaving the high-control group? How specifically has that manifested for you? · · · · · · 117
How has shunning or disconnection affected you? · · · · · · 119
How can you help yourself cope with this cruel tactic? · · · · · · 120
What steps have you taken to rebuild community and make new connections for yourself? · · · · · · 122
What other steps could you take to rebuild and nourish a circle of friendship for yourself? · · · · · · 123

The Invitation Within Suffering (The Challenge to Heal, Chapter 29, page 219) · · · · · · 124
How successful have you been in using suffering as a vehicle to discover further levels of growth or awakening? · · · · · · 124
Have you been able to use this experience of manipulation, deception and exploitation as a teacher? What has this high-control experience taught you? · · · · · · 126

How Do I Proceed From Here? (The Challenge to Heal, Chapter 30, page 221) · · · · · · 130
How have you used the Zen question *"This being the case, how do I proceed from here?"* to help you rebuild your life? Explain how you *have*, or how you *intend to* move forward. · · · · · · 130
Are you now able to see that you are the hero of your own life? Explain. For example, describe some of the things you are proud of with regard to your leave-taking experience. (See Chapter 4 in *The Challenge to Heal*) · · · · · · 132
Describe how you are now claiming sovereignty over your life? How does that feel? · · · · · · 134
How do you celebrate this awesome accomplishment? · · · · · · 134
What questions have you encountered in the midst of your suffering due to manipulation and exploitation? · · · · · · 136
How have you been able to use these questions to help your recovery and growth? · · · · · · 136

The Challenge of Forgiveness (The Challenge to Heal, Chapter 31, page 224) · · · · · · 139
What are your feelings about forgiveness, with regard to what happened to you in the high-control group or relationship? Where are you in relationship to embracing the need to forgive? · · · · · · 139

There Must Be A Pony (The Challenge to Heal, Chapter 32, page 228) · · · · · · 141
What value (benefits) have you discovered in the midst of your suffering? · · · · · · 141
What would you want family and friends to know about this entire experience of exploitation in a high-control group or relationship? · · · · · · 144

Recommended Reading Section (The Challenge to Heal, page 231) · **146**
What books do you still want to read to help with your recovery from being exploited in a
high-control group? · 146

Alternative Healing Modalities (The Challenge to Heal, page 235) · **147**
Have you used any of these alternative therapies (or others) to help with your recovery from control
abuse? How has that worked? · 147

What is next for you? · **149**
What is your vision for your life now? · 150
Have you developed specific goals that will help you realize your vision? Outline them here. · · · · · · · · · · · · · 152
Have you developed concrete steps to reach those goals? (You can outline the steps you intend
to take on a few different goals on the next few pages.) · 154

**Summarize what you have learned about yourself and life, due to the entire experience
of being *in* a high-control group and getting *out* of a high-control group.** · **156**

PART 2 Feelings Journal Guidelines ·159
Feelings Journal Pages · 160-211

PART 3 Extra Pages · 213-234

Part 1

Guidelines for Documenting Your High-Control Group Story

"One way to take care of ourselves during the challenging second change stage of personal reactions, chaos, confusion, uncertainty, lack of control and pain is to find ways to tell the story of the abuse and its effects. As members of an extremist cult, terrorist group, religious commune, etc. we were subjected to mind-control, undue influence, demands for silence, threats of death, threats of banishment from the tribe, and many other disturbing experiences. This sort of relentless stress is traumatic and needs to be named and told, to release it and reflect upon what has been learned from it.

Psychiatrist Judith Lewis Herman tells us, "The conflict between the will to deny horrible events and the will to proclaim them aloud is the central dialectic of psychological trauma." Since we are rarely able to "proclaim them aloud", one safe way to break the enforced silence of oppressive groups and speak about the sometimes unspeakable abuses and losses, is to record them in a private journal.

… Judith Lewis Herman's second stage of recovery from trauma is called, "remembrance and mourning". One way to remember and mourn is by journaling. I sometimes like to insert a hyphen in the word remember as it applies to healing trauma. As we re-member, we put the pieces of ourselves (our 'members'), shattered by trauma, back together again. Don't discount the importance of re-membering. Begin to put yourself back together by journaling.

Former high-control group members have experienced profound stress and trauma in so many ways – while in the group, while trying to extricate themselves from it, and while working to recover from it. Unfortunately there is no formal critical-incident debriefing or story-telling circle for brave mind-control escapees - unless they can afford to go to a therapist. If you cannot afford therapy right now – or even if you can – you can reap the benefits of writing down the details of your story.

One way to tell your story is to create a private journal dedicated to documenting the narrative of your undue influence odyssey. In a journal you can:

- Make a record of your life as a recruit, a member and a defector, (chronological or not)
- Record all the details of both mundane and traumatizing events
- Record how you were treated (influenced, persuaded, deceived, coerced, manipulated, rewarded, threatened, pacified, punished, etc.)
- Journal about emotions (pain, fear, anger, guilt) that still grip you.
- Write about all the sacrifices you had to make
- Write about the friends you made, valued … and lost
- Reflect on all you have lost by being a member of the group

- *Write about things you were pressured to do but did not want to do*
- *Write about the personal hurts, the insults, the degradations*
- *Include any good experiences (there must be some)*
- *Write about ways you intend to take care of yourself now*
- *Write down dreams/goals you have for your future, now that you are free*
- *Journal about what you learned from the entire experience, not so much the ideology, but more what you learned from being controlled, from being exploited, from suppressing your feelings, from discovering the deceptions, from being placed in double-bind, catch-22 situations, from daring to leave, etc. Just record what you can … when you can …*
- *Do not worry about finding or articulating the 'why' for everything. For now, simply record the 'what' and 'how' you felt about it - don't worry about finding a 'why', an explanation, a reason for everything. Down the road, you may discover "the why" … you may not. That is just the way it is. In life there are often no definitive answers to the question why?*

Journaling about your experience is a valid and extremely helpful form of psychological release, affirmation and healing. When you do it for yourself, you don't have to worry about chronological order or providing a detailed context (unless you want to). You don't have to wonder if you are explaining it well enough for someone else (e.g. a therapist) to understand. You are doing it for yourself, so do it in any form you choose. Just do it! You may decide to do it as an art journal using stencils, paint, markers, photos, or collage materials. There is no right or wrong way. There is just your unique way.

If you find it difficult to write about your experiences, just do what you can, as you can – you don't want journaling to become another source of stress. You can begin by simply recording the topics (headings) you will write about at some point. Then, as you feel able, pick and choose which topic you feel able to write about in more detail. This is not a test. You do not have to hand it over for someone else to read. No one will be looking over your shoulder and grading you. And … try not to judge and grade yourself. Your main job right now is to take gentle, loving care of yourself by releasing your story onto the open, non-judgmental page." Excerpted from The Challenge to Heal, Chapter 11, "Documenting Your Story", pages 54 - 60

As you progress through the difficult parts of telling your story and begin to enjoy the healing benefits of so doing, eventually your personal narrative will become a celebration of life – your new life – free of coercive controls and interference. In a way, this document of the story of your abuse in a high-control group is like an intimate love letter to yourself. A love letter in that - amidst the account of the disempowerment and pain, you acknowledge and appreciate the person who survived it, and honor all that you have accomplished by claiming freedom. As you document the story of your exploited past, you will begin to enjoy moments of satisfaction and contentment in the present and glimpses into the future – one that will be of your design and of your making.

When we have spent time in high-control groups that required us to suppress and repress our authentic self, taking time to document the experience is one way to discover what drew us into the group, what kept us there, what prompted us to consider leaving, how we managed the leave-taking and the toll that all of that took on our body/mind. As we document our story we will rediscover who we are, what we value, what we think, what we need, what we want – creating a way to peel back the layers of inauthenticity we had to create to protect ourselves from so much undue interference. As we document, we will finally discover our true self waiting to emerge. What a joy!

So … time to begin to compose the story of your unique experience in a high-control situation. There is no one particular way in which to do this. With the prompts on each page of this workbook you can begin where you like and jump around as you like. There is no requirement to document your story in a linear fashion.

Although many of us may have a preference to document or journal on our computer, it does not have the same power as writing by hand on paper. Writing by hand allows a closer connection to and release of the energies in your body. It is a more intimate, personal experience. Journaling by hand allows you to scratch things out, scribble notes in the margin, and add design elements using markers, paints or collage elements.

Down the road when you look back at this workbook, the things you scratch out may prove to hold some very interesting and illuminating information for you – perhaps being things you were not yet able to admit to yourself or own.

Consider this workbook as a draft. Down the road if you want a formal, typewritten version of your story you can use the material developed in this workbook as the basis to create a 'final' print version.

Assuming that you have already read *The Challenge to Heal* book, it is now time to stop reading my words and begin to write your own! This workbook is designed to help facilitate that process. Just let it be your recovery companion and it will guide you through the process. If you find that not enough space is allotted for your response to a particular 'prompt', there are numbered blank pages at the end of the workbook section that you can use to elaborate. Just be sure to reference the page numbers at the back of the section to the original page where you began your thoughts and vice versa.

Don't worry if certain portions of the book remain blank for a while. Write as you remember and as you feel inclined to record the various elements of your story. You are not only creating a written record of what happened to you, but you are also engaged in a therapeutic debriefing process that helps your body/mind heal and come to terms with what happened and who you are now.

Part 2 of this book, from pages 160-211, is a dedicated **Feelings Journal** in which you will record the most challenging feelings you are experiencing each day. Guidelines for how to use the Feelings Journal are found on page 159.

Part 3 of this book from pages 213 to 234 of this book are **Extra Pages** for you to use if you do not have enough space to document aspects of your story or to express your feelings. Be sure to cross-reference the pages so you can easily access the related pages.

"As the number of studies increased, it became clear that writing was a far more powerful tool for healing than anyone had ever imagined." James W. Pennebaker

"When you get to the end of all the light you know
and it's time to step into the darkness of the unknown,
faith is knowing that one of two things shall happen:
either you will be given something solid to stand on,
or you will be taught how to fly."

Edward Teller

Document your history in the high-control group.

How did you get involved with the high-control group that unduly influenced you? How did it all begin?

_____
_____
_____
_____
_____
_____
_____
_____
_____
_____
_____
_____
_____
_____
_____
_____
_____
_____
_____
_____
_____
_____

"Writing is a form of therapy; sometimes I wonder how all those who do not write, compose, or paint can manage to escape the madness, melancholia, the panic and fear which is inherent in a human situation." Graham Greene

"I was mortified by the prospect of becoming hopelessly trapped in someone else's story." — Lionel Shriver

What was your daily/weekly life like as a member of a high-control group?

"Don't trust your memory, jot it all down." — *Earl Schoaff*

"Most of us are awakened, some more and some less brutally, to the fact that people often do not mean what they say or say the opposite of what they mean. And not only "people," but the very people we trusted most - our parents, teachers, leaders." Erich Fromm

Document some of your specific experiences and relationships in the high-control group – ones that were rewarding, and ones that disturbed you.

"Write what disturbs you, what you fear, what you have not been willing to speak about. Be willing to be split open."
Natalie Goldberg

"Your pain is the breaking of the shell that encloses your understanding." Kahlil Gibran

"Absolute faith corrupts as absolutely as absolute power." Eric Hoffer

What controls and pressures did you experience?

"You can chain me, you can torture me, you can even destroy this body, but you will never imprison my mind."
Mahatma Gandhi

"Control the manner in which a man interprets his world, and you have gone a long way toward controlling his behavior." Stanley Milgram

"Experience is not what happens to you. It is what you do with what happens to you." Aldous Huxley

What thoughts, feelings, needs, desires, longings, impulses or actions did you have to suppress to survive in the controlling group?

"That of which we are not aware, owns us." James Hollis

"Every man's condition is a solution in hieroglyphic to those inquires which he would make; he lives it as life before he perceives it as truth." Ralph Waldo Emerson

Are there things that happened in the high-control milieu that you never told anyone and you want to record here?

"Those who can make you believe absurdities, can make you commit atrocities." Voltaire

"Should you shield the canyons from the windstorms you would never see the true beauty of their carvings." Elizabeth Kubler-Ross

"Happy is the man who has broken the chains which hurt the mind, and has given up worrying once and for all. Be patient and tough; one day this pain will be useful to you." Ovid, Metamorphoses

Describe the thoughts and/or incidents that caused you to question and doubt the high-control group and your involvement with it:

___

"In the midst of winter, I finally learned that there was in me an invincible summer." Albert Camus

"Doubt is unsettling to the ego, and those who are drawn to ideologies that promise the dispelling of doubt by proffering certainties will never grow. In seeking certainty they are courting the death of the soul, whose nature is forever churning possibility, forever seeking the larger, forever riding the melting edge of certainty's glacier."   James Hollis

"It is the first responsibility of every citizen to question authority." Benjamin Franklin

How did you handle the doubts and cope with the questions about whether you might be in a destructive group? What did you feel at that time?

"One's destination is never a place, but rather a new way of looking at things." Henry Miller

"If all you can do is crawl, start crawling." Rumi

What resources or information helped you to begin to think about leaving, or did you have to figure it all out on your own? Explain.

"The essence of the independent mind lies not in what it thinks, but in how it thinks." Christopher Hitchens

"Writing is medicine. It is an appropriate antidote to injury. It is an appropriate companion for any difficult change." Julia Cameron

What concerns or fears did you have about leaving? How did they affect your ability to leave? How did you overcome them?

"Some changes look negative on the surface but you will soon realize that space is being created in your life for something new to emerge." Eckhart Tolle

"If a fear cannot be articulated, it can't be conquered."   Stephen King

"The fears we cannot climb become our walls.   Noah Ben Shea

"The cave you fear to enter holds the treasure you seek."   Joseph Campbell

How did your actual leaving of the high-control group unfold?

"There is freedom waiting for you,
On the breezes of the sky,
And you ask "What if I fall?"
Oh but my darling,
What if you fly?"
Erin Hanson

"To find out who rules over you, simply find out who you are not allowed to criticize." Kevin Alfred Strom

"It is easier, far easier, to obey another than to command oneself." Irvin D. Yalom

What were your experiences and feelings once you left?

"Things falling apart is a kind of testing and also a kind of healing. We think that the point is to pass the test or to overcome the problem, but the truth is that things don't really get solved. They come together and they fall apart ... The healing comes from letting there be room for all of this to happen: room for grief, for relief, for misery, for joy." Pema Chodron

"Leaving a place, a person or a country silently and without any notice is a heroic and a noble way of teaching the importance of your presence to those who ignore your existence." Mehmet Murat Ildan

"The creative members of an orthodoxy, any orthodoxy, ultimately outgrow their disciplines."   Irvin D. Yalom

Did you find yourself in a grieving process? How did you express your grief?

"You must do the thing you think you cannot do." Eleanor Roosevelt

"One can choose to go back toward safety or forward toward growth. Growth must be chosen again and again; fear must be overcome again and again." Abraham Maslow

"Whenever sacred duty decays and chaos prevails, then I create myself." Bhagavad Gita

Where do you stand now in relationship to the group that exploited you? How do you feel about that?

"The devil can cite Scripture for his purpose." William Shakespeare

"I chose a life apart from the common flow, not only because the common flow makes me sick but because I question the logic of the flow, and not only that - I don't know if the flow exists! Why should I chain myself to the wheel when the wheel itself might be a construct, an invention, a common dream to enslave us?"   Steve Toltz

What hurts, indignities, wounds are still needing to be addressed? How are you dealing with them now?

"Write hard and clear about what hurts." Ernest Hemingway

"Observing, recording, and preserving the memory of both the large and small events of life is one of the oldest and most satisfying ways to bring order to consciousness." Mihali Csikzentmihalyi

Who are you now, in spite of the pain – beyond the influence of the group and the pain it caused?

"Many of us spend our whole lives running from feeling with the mistaken belief that you cannot bear the pain. But you have already borne the pain. What you have not done is feel all you are beyond that pain." Kahlil Gibran

"What happens to us is not as important as the meaning we assign to it. Journaling helps sort this out."
Michael Hyatt

How do you take care of yourself? How do you calm or soothe yourself? Are there things you have been intending to do to help yourself, but have not done yet?

"It's common to reject or punish yourself when you've been rejected by others. When you experience disappointment from the way your family or others treat you, that's the time to take special care of yourself. What are you doing to nurture yourself? What are you doing to protect yourself? Find a healthy way to express your pain." Christina Enevoldsen

Have you used psychotherapy to help deal with your wounds? How did it help? What did you learn?

"Everyone has the right to freedom of opinion and expression; this right includes freedom to hold opinions without interference and to seek, receive and impart information and ideas through any media and regardless of frontiers."   United Nations, Universal Declaration of Human Rights

"The after-effects of being in a high-control group, a repressive cult, or an abusive relationship are many. Some effects such as anxiety, loneliness, depression, anger and low self-esteem can really affect your quality of life. When symptoms seem prolonged or overly intense, it may be time to consider finding a good psychotherapist. A therapist will accompany you through the process of grieving your losses, help you find ways to manage your symptoms and help you envision ways to rebuild a new life." The Challenge to Heal, page 200

If you have not been able to use therapy, what are your concerns about it? (Please revisit Chapter 28 in The Challenge to Heal book, page 200)

"The world breaks everyone, and afterward some are strong at the broken places." Ernest Hemingway, Farewell to Arms

Are you aware of your current wants and needs? Describe them.

"Turning away from what you're afraid of isn't the same as turning toward what you want. What do you want?
Dawna Markova

"And now that you don't have to be perfect, you can be good." John Steinbeck

Have you noticed a shift in your values since leaving? Explain.

"To be mature you have to realize what you value most... Not to arrive at a clear understanding of one's own values is a tragic waste. You have missed the whole point of what life is for." Eleanor Roosevelt

"Mature adults gravitate toward new values and understandings, not just rehashing and blind acceptance of past patterns and previous learning. This is an ongoing process and maturity demands lifelong learners."
David W. Earle

Why People Join and Stay in High-Control Groups
(The Challenge to Heal, Chapter 6, page 25)

Why do you think you joined or stayed in your high-control group or relationship?

_____
_____
_____
_____
_____
_____
_____
_____
_____
_____
_____
_____
_____
_____
_____
_____
_____
_____
_____
_____
_____

"The nature of psychological compulsion is such that those who act under constraint remain under the impression that they are acting on their own initiative. The victim of mind-manipulation does not know that he is a victim. To him the walls of his prison are invisible, and he believes himself to be free. That he is not free is apparent only to other people. His servitude is strictly objective."   Aldous Huxley

How will you attend to the particular need or inclination that pulled you into a destructive group or relationship, so that you do not become vulnerable to any further manipulation and exploitation?

"I realize that if I were stable, prudent and static, I'd live in death. Therefore I accept confusion, uncertainty, fear and emotional ups and downs; because that's the price I'm willing to pay for a fluid, perplexed and exciting life."
Carl Rogers

What is to Be Gained by Leaving?
(The Challenge to Heal, Chapter 7, page 38)

What specifically have you gained by exiting the high-control group or relationship?

_____
_____
_____
_____
_____
_____
_____
_____
_____
_____
_____
_____
_____
_____
_____
_____
_____
_____
_____
_____
_____
_____
_____
_____

"New beginnings are often disguised as painful endings." — Lao Tzu

"A kind of light spread out from her. And everything changed color. And the world opened out. And a day was good to awaken to. And there were no limits to anything. And the people of the world were good and handsome. And I was not afraid anymore." John Steinbeck

Conversely, what challenges have you had to face because of leaving a high-control group?

"We know that we will have to burn to the ground in one way or another and then sit right in the ashes of who we once thought we were and go on from there." Clarissa Pinkola Estes

"Perhaps the biggest tragedy of our lives is that freedom is possible, yet we can pass our years trapped in the same old patterns...We may want to love other people without holding back, to feel authentic, to breathe in the beauty around us, to dance and sing. Yet each day we listen to inner voices that keep our life small."   Tara Brach

Stages of Change
(The Challenge to Heal, Chapter 10, page 50)

What stage do you think you are in in your transition? Describe it?

___

"The only real battle in life is between hanging on and letting go." Shannon L. Adler

Based on Chapter 10 in *The Challenge to Heal Book*, what do you need to do to move into the next stage of change?

"Who am I? ... Am I irrevocably shaped by the circumstance of my personal history, or am I still free to move and grow, to uncover a new and brighter path?" Wayne Muller

The Challenge of Becoming Comfortable with Feelings
(The Challenge to Heal, Chapter 12, page 61)

How comfortable are you in dealing with difficult feelings? What feelings have been most present for you since leaving the high-control group?

_____
_____
_____
_____
_____
_____
_____
_____
_____
_____
_____
_____
_____
_____
_____
_____
_____
_____
_____
_____

"It is the place of feeling that binds us or frees us. 'Free' is not free from feelings, but free to feel each one and let it move on, unafraid of the movement of life." — Jack Kornfield

"Letting go means to come to the realization that some people are a part of your history, but not a part of your destiny." Steve Maraboli

A Closer Look at the Most Challenging Feelings
(The Challenge to Heal, Chapter 13, page 66)

Which of the feelings addressed in Chapter 13 of the book is most challenging for you, and why?

_____
_____
_____
_____
_____
_____
_____
_____
_____
_____
_____
_____
_____
_____
_____
_____
_____
_____
_____
_____
_____
_____

"Once connection to consciousness is made and reacted to, the trauma and pain become a historical fact instead of a continuous force." Arthur Janov, M.D.

"The facts (and feelings) of one's life are far less important than how we remember them, how we have internalized them and are driven by them, or how we are able to work with them." James Hollis

What can you do about these challenging feelings (based on what you read in The Challenge to Heal, pages 66-81)?

"None are more hopelessly enslaved than those who falsely believe they are free."   Johann Wolfgang von Goethe

Challenge Thoughts of Suicide
(The Challenge to Heal, Chapter 14, page 82)

Have the aftereffects of leaving a high-control group ever caused you to contemplate ending your life? Describe.

_____
_____
_____
_____
_____
_____
_____
_____
_____
_____
_____
_____
_____
_____
_____
_____
_____
_____
_____
_____
_____

"These destructive thoughts seem to have a life of their own and are not unlike an extremist group trying to recruit you for a suicide mission – but in this case it wants you to be both the terrorist and the victim." The Challenge to Heal, page 83

What are your current thoughts about suicide (after reading Chapter 14, pages 82-86 in The Challenge to Heal?)

"Suffering is part of our training program for becoming wise." Ram Dass

"Courage is the price life exacts for granting us peace." Amelia Earhart

"Anger is the prelude to courage." Eric Hoffer

Dis-identify From Negative Beliefs, Thoughts, Feelings
(The Challenge to Heal, Chapter 15, page 87)

What are the beliefs/thoughts/feelings that are most troubling for you now?

_____
_____
_____
_____
_____
_____
_____
_____
_____
_____
_____
_____
_____
_____
_____
_____
_____
_____
_____
_____
_____
_____
_____

"Relate TO the belief, thought, feeling or ego-state, not FROM it." The Challenge to Heal, page 89

"To attain true inner freedom, you must be able to objectively watch your problems instead of being lost in them."
Michael A. Singer

How are you doing with the dis-identification technique, page 89? (It's a powerful tool and one that will serve you well throughout your life - once you incorporate it into your repertoire of healing skills.)

"Learn to watch your drama unfold while at the same time knowing you are more than your drama." — Ram Dass

"Reject your sense of injury and the injury itself disappears." Marcus Aurelius

Emotions Manifesting As Physical Ailments
(The Challenge to Heal, Chapter 16, page 93)

What has been your experience with physical ailments, possibly due to being in a high-control group?

___

"Repressed material, buried by the unconscious, eventually tries to come to conscious awareness in order to be processed, integrated or released. If we refuse to, or cannot pay attention, the repressed material will sometimes manifest as a physical ailment - which often uncannily symbolizes the repressed contents of the unconscious." The Challenge to Heal, page 93

"I promise you nothing is as chaotic as it seems. Nothing is worth diminishing your health. Nothing is worth poisoning yourself into stress, anxiety, and fear." Steve Maraboli

"Recent studies of mindfulness practices reveal that they can result in profound improvements in a range of physiological, mental, and interpersonal domains in our lives. Cardiac, endocrine, and immune functions are improved with mindfulness practices. Empathy, compassion, and interpersonal sensitivity seem to be improved. People who come to develop the capacity to pay attention in the present moment without grasping on to their inevitable judgments also develop a deeper sense of well-being and what can be considered a form of mental coherence."   Daniel J. Siegel

Accepting Life As It Unfolds
(The Challenge to Heal,
Chapter 17, page 99)

How often do you find yourself fighting against or resisting the flow of life or "what is"?

_____
_____
_____
_____
_____
_____
_____
_____
_____
_____
_____
_____
_____
_____
_____
_____
_____
_____
_____
_____
_____

"It is important to expect nothing, to take every experience, including the negative ones, as merely steps on the path, and to proceed." Ram Dass

Do you still view yourself as a victim of the high-control group or relationship due to the controls and coercion?

What can you do to move from victim to hero of your own story? (See pages 101-104, The Challenge to Heal)

"The only way to live is by accepting each minute as an unrepeatable miracle." Tara Brach

"If we take each teaching, each loss, each gain, each fear, each joy as it arises and experience it fully, life becomes workable. We are no longer a "victim of life." And then every experience, even the loss of our dearest one, becomes another opportunity for awakening."   Stephen Levine

"We have only to follow the thread of the hero path ... Where we had thought to travel outward, we will come to the center of ourselves. And where we had thought to be alone, we will be with all the world." Joseph Campbell

Who Are You Now, Without the Controls?
(The Challenge to Heal, Chapter 18, page 105)

Did you have to build a false self to survive in the group? Explain.

"I see my life as an unfolding set of opportunities to awaken." Ram Dass

"The hardest arithmetic to master is that which enables us to count our blessings." Eric Hoffer

How are you doing now in reclaiming your authentic identity?

"No matter how awakened you are, the conditioning roots are deep; very deep. Reclamation is a constant process."
Bryant McGill

"One of the greatest regrets in life is being what others would want you to be, rather than being yourself." Shannon L. Alder

The Challenge of Guilt
(The Challenge to Heal,
Chapter 19, page 111)

Have you been able to determine if you are carrying any shame or guilt due to the controls and coercion? Based on what you read in Chapter 19, what kind of guilt are you dealing with?

_____
_____
_____
_____
_____
_____
_____
_____
_____
_____
_____
_____
_____
_____
_____
_____
_____
_____
_____
_____
_____
_____

What are your feelings about what you learned about "existential guilt"?

"Some of our malaise as a follower of a destructive group may have been due to the existential guilt of not being able to be authentic, not being free to be our self and reach for our individual potential." The Challenge to Heal, page 111

"Guilt is a terrible burden to carry. Whatever you did that you are not proud of, you were doing the best you knew how – at that moment – to survive. To heal, you must release the burden of guilt and the ensuing pain. You must offer yourself understanding and forgiveness. Can you begin that process now?" Bonnie Zieman

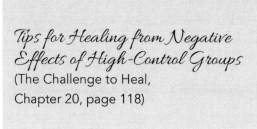

Tips for Healing from Negative Effects of High-Control Groups
(The Challenge to Heal, Chapter 20, page 118)

Which tips from The Challenge to Heal, pages 118-154 have been most helpful for you?

___

"Some changes look negative on the surface but you will soon realize that space is being created in your life for something new to emerge." Eckhart Tolle

"Through loyalty to the past, our mind refuses to realize that tomorrow's joy is possible only if today's makes way for it; that each wave owes the beauty of its line to the withdrawal of the receding one." — André Gide

Which tips do you still need to incorporate into your repertoire of healing tools? What is difficult about this for you?

"Sometimes letting things go is an act of far greater power than defending or hanging on." — Eckhart Tolle

"Challenge yourself to step out of the limits of black/white, either/or thinking. Embrace the privilege of discovering all the beautiful shades of grey between those extreme, binary points of view. Challenge yourself to embrace an open, creative approach to life rather than a closed, limited approach. You will be entranced and excited by the range of possibilities that open up to you." The Challenge to Heal, page 142

Psychosocial Development Impeded By Imposed Controls
(The Challenge to Heal, Chapter 21, page 157)

How might your normal development into a mature, capable adult have been interrupted by being in a high-control group (The Challenge to Heal, pages 157-165)?

_____
_____
_____
_____
_____
_____
_____
_____
_____
_____
_____
_____
_____
_____
_____
_____
_____
_____
_____
_____
_____

"If you plan on being anything less than you are capable of being, you will probably be unhappy all the days of your life." Abraham Maslow

What stages of development do you most need to address and incorporate now (trust, autonomy, initiative, industry, authentic identity, intimacy, caring, wisdom)?

"Growth occurs when individuals confront problems, struggle to master them, and through that struggle develop new aspects of their skills, capacities, views about life." Carl Rogers

"When you are denied the right to exercise your own initiative, to ask questions, to determine your own purpose in life, to initiate your own plans and see them through to completion, you never have the pleasure or experience of feeling free, autonomous or authentic. Nor do you develop the full capacity of courage that comes with completing independent initiatives." *The Challenge to Heal, page 162*

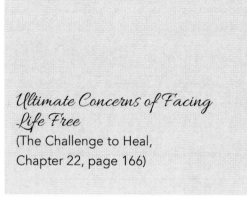

Ultimate Concerns of Facing Life Free
(The Challenge to Heal, Chapter 22, page 166)

How did you feel after reading the chapter on the existential givens (life's ultimate concerns) in The Challenge to Heal?

_____
_____
_____
_____
_____
_____
_____
_____
_____
_____
_____
_____
_____
_____
_____
_____
_____
_____
_____
_____
_____
_____

"A deep existential anxiety crisis precedes the final integration of the Self." Thomas Merton

How might you have used membership in a high-control group to avoid the basic givens (aloneness, mortality, freedom/responsibility, meaning) of any human life?

How will you help yourself to confront these ultimate concerns of life now?

"Anxiety is the dizziness of freedom." Soren Kierkegaard

Self-Love & Self-Acceptance – Essential to Healing
(The Challenge to Heal, Chapter 23, page 174)

How are you doing in the areas of self-acceptance and self-love now?

"If I could distill all of what I've learned from the study of psychology, my experience as a therapist, my experience exiting a cult and adapting once out, and an on-going love affair with certain aspects of Eastern philosophy into one summary sentence, it would simply be: Love and accept yourself. Everything else falls into place from there." Bonnie Zieman, The Challenge to Heal, pages 175

"On this sacred path of radical acceptance, rather than striving for perfection, we discover how to love ourselves into wholeness." Tara Brach

Are you using the **E**motional **F**reedom **T**echnique acupressure rubbing technique described in Chapter 23 of *The Challenge to Heal*?

How have you adapted the EFT statement (used while you rub the tender spot on your chest) to fit *your* needs? (*Even with the fact that _____fill in the blank_____, I deeply and completely love, accept and forgive myself.*)

_____
_____
_____
_____
_____
_____
_____
_____
_____
_____
_____
_____
_____
_____
_____
_____
_____
_____
_____
_____
_____
_____
_____
_____
_____
_____
_____
_____

"The curious paradox is that when I accept myself just as I am, then I can change." Carl R. Rogers

"Pain is not wrong. Reacting to pain as wrong initiates the trance of unworthiness. The moment we believe something is wrong, our world shrinks and we lose ourselves in the effort to combat the pain." Tara Brach

Self-Acceptance Awakens a Sense of Belonging
(The Challenge to Heal, Chapter 24, page 183)

How are you doing with creating a sense of belonging in your own heart?

_____

"When you accept and love yourself, you create a belonging place within. You open your heart to yourself. You create a sense of belonging in your own heart – a place you can always turn to and find non-judgmental, open arms metaphorically waiting to welcome you." The Challenge to Heal, page 183

"The trance of unworthiness keeps the sweetness of belonging out of reach. The path to "the sweetness of belonging" is acceptance – acceptance of ourselves and acceptance of others without judgment." Tara Brach

Creative Visualization –
A Healing Resource
(The Challenge to Heal,
Chapter 25, page 186)

Have you used guided meditations to help with your healing? How have you adapted meditations for your particular circumstances?

"Imagination is more important than knowledge." Albert Einstein

Acting As If
(The Challenge to Heal,
Chapter 26, page 192)

What do you think about "acting as if" as a technique to help with your recovery from undue controls? How have you employed it?

"Imagine for yourself a character, a model personality, whose example you determine to follow, in private as well as in public." Epictetus

Embracing Other Movements, Groups or Religions
(The Challenge to Heal, Chapter 27, page 197)

What were your thoughts/reactions when you read this chapter about taking some time before joining other movements or groups?

_____

"Give yourself time to experience all the losses involved in leaving one belief system and to grieve those losses before you muddy the fresh internal waters with new beliefs and more external expectations." The Challenge to Heal, page 198

Where do you stand with regard to gurus, causes, leaders, movements, god, religion, etc.?

"The important thing is not to stop questioning." Albert Einstein

The Challenge of Ostracism
(The Challenge to Heal,
Chapter 29, page 211)

Have you been cut off, alienated, shunned or disconnected from or by family and friends due to leaving the high-control group? How specifically has that manifested for you?

_____
_____
_____
_____
_____
_____
_____
_____
_____
_____
_____
_____
_____
_____
_____
_____
_____
_____
_____
_____

"There are few things in life that are as shaming, hurtful and personally destructive as being rejected, excluded, left out, shunned or ostracized. One cannot help but wonder if those who do the shunning truly understand what a vile act it is." The Challenge to Heal, page 211

"People are never so completely and enthusiastically evil as when they act out of religious conviction." Umberto Eco

How has shunning or disconnection affected you?

"Look at how I was wounded in the house of those who loved me." Zechariah 13:6

How can you help yourself cope with this cruel tactic?

"The loyalty of the true believer is to the whole —the church, party, nation —and not to his fellow true believer." Eric Hoffer

"Life does not accommodate you, it shatters you ... Every seed destroys its container or else there would be no fruition."
Florida Scott-Maxwell

What steps have you taken to rebuild community and make new connections for yourself?

"Being able to feel safe with other people is probably the single most important aspect of mental health; safe connections are fundamental to meaningful and satisfying lives." Bessel A. van der Kolk, M.D.

What other steps could you take to rebuild and nourish a circle of friendship for yourself?

"We may want to love other people without holding back, to feel authentic, to breathe in the beauty around us, to dance and sing. Yet each day we listen to inner voices that keep our life small." Tara Brach

The Invitation Within Suffering
(The Challenge to Heal, Chapter 29, page 219)

How successful have you been in using suffering as a vehicle to discover further levels of growth or awakening?

_____
_____
_____
_____
_____
_____
_____
_____
_____
_____
_____
_____
_____
_____
_____
_____
_____
_____
_____

"For most people, their spiritual teacher is their suffering, because eventually the suffering brings about awakening." Eckhart Tolle

"Radical acceptance rests on letting go of the illusion of control and a willingness to notice and accept things as they are right now, without judging ... Acceptance is the only way out of hell." Marsha M. Linehan

Have you been able to use this experience of manipulation, deception and exploitation as a teacher? What has this high-control experience taught you?

_____
_____
_____
_____
_____
_____
_____
_____
_____
_____
_____
_____
_____
_____
_____
_____
_____
_____
_____
_____
_____
_____
_____
_____
_____
_____
_____
_____

"Who taught you all this, Doctor?" The reply came promptly. "Suffering." Albert Camus

"Treat the past as a school." Jim Rohn

"This is what I have learned: Within the sorrow, there is grace. When we come close to those things that break us down, we touch those things that also break us open. And in that breaking open, we uncover our true nature ... This is the point of healing: When we have told the story, we can leave the story behind. What remains is a hidden wholeness, alive and unbroken." Wayne Muller

"Ruin is a gift. Ruin is the road to transformation." Elizabeth Gilbert

"Take the risk of thinking for yourself, much more happiness, truth, beauty, and wisdom will come to you that way."
Christopher Hitchens

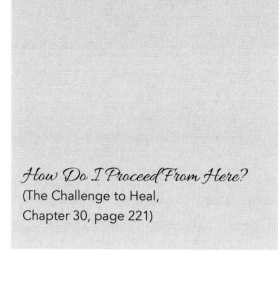

How Do I Proceed From Here?
(The Challenge to Heal, Chapter 30, page 221)

How have you used the Zen question *"This being the case, how do I proceed from here?"* to help you rebuild your life? Explain how you *have*, or how you *intend to* move forward.

_____
_____
_____
_____
_____
_____
_____
_____
_____
_____
_____
_____
_____
_____
_____
_____
_____
_____
_____
_____
_____
_____

"The greatest weapon against stress is our ability to choose one thought over another." William James

"But you do not need anybody's permission to move on with your life. It does not matter whether or not those responsible for harming you ever understand what they did, care about what they did, or apologize for it. It does not matter. All that matters is your ability to stop fondling the experience with your brain. Which you can do right now." Augusten Burroughs

Are you now able to see that you are the hero of your own life? Explain. For example, describe some of the things you are proud of with regard to your leave-taking experience. (See Chapter 4 in *The Challenge to Heal*)

"To do the best you can, for yourself, for the moment, while simultaneously knowing and feeling pain, without becoming cynical, helpless, or paralyzed by fear of the pain, is the task of the hero." Susanna McMahon

"Try again. Fail again. Fail better."   Samuel Beckett

Describe how you are now claiming sovereignty over your life? How does that feel? How do you celebrate this awesome accomplishment?

"Isn't it marvelous to discover that you're the one you've been waiting for? That you are your own freedom?" Byron Katie

"We have the seed of everything in us, and we have to seize the situation in our hand, to recover our own sovereignty."
Tich Nhat Hanh

What questions have you encountered in the midst of your suffering due to manipulation and exploitation? How have you been able to use these questions to help your recovery and growth?

*"Do I dare
Disturb the universe?"*
T.S. Eliot

"It's the questions we can't answer that teach us the most. They teach us how to think. If you give a man an answer, all he gains is a little fact. But give him a question and he'll look for his own answers." Patrick Rothfuss

"It is the pull of opposite poles that stretches souls. And only stretched souls make music." Eric Hoffer

The Challenge of Forgiveness
(The Challenge to Heal,
Chapter 31, page 224)

What are your feelings about forgiveness, with regard to what happened to you in the high-control group or relationship? Where are you in relationship to embracing the need to forgive?

_____
_____
_____
_____
_____
_____
_____
_____
_____
_____
_____
_____
_____
_____
_____
_____
_____
_____
_____
_____
_____
_____

"When we forgive, the slave we free is ourselves." — Edward M. Hallowell

"Live like a tree, giving, forgiving and free." Debasish Mridha

There Must Be A Pony
(The Challenge to Heal, Chapter 32, page 228)

What value (benefits) have you discovered in the midst of your suffering?

_____
_____
_____
_____
_____
_____
_____
_____
_____
_____
_____
_____
_____
_____
_____
_____
_____
_____
_____
_____

"Life has no meaning a priori ... It is up to you to give it a meaning, and value is nothing but the meaning that you choose." Jean-Paul Sartre

"Embrace the challenge to focus on all the learnings, all the gifts and the many wonderful possibilities contained within your hard-won freedom and not only on the suffering that came with it." *The Challenge to Heal, page 229*

"Every moment of one's existence one is growing into more or retreating into less. One is always living a little more or dying a little bit." Norman Mailer

What would you want family and friends to know about this entire experience of exploitation in a high-control group or relationship?

_____
_____
_____
_____
_____
_____
_____
_____
_____
_____
_____
_____
_____
_____
_____
_____
_____
_____
_____
_____
_____
_____
_____
_____
_____
_____
_____

"Do not indoctrinate your children. Teach them how to think for themselves, how to evaluate evidence, and how to disagree with you." — Richard Dawkins

"... suffering smashes to pieces the complacency of our normal fictions about reality, and forces us to become alive in a special sense – to see carefully, to feel deeply, to touch ourselves and our world in ways we have heretofore avoided. It has been said, and truly I think, that suffering is the first grace." Ken Wilber

Recommended Reading Section
(The Challenge to Heal, page 231)

What books do you still want to read to help with your recovery from being exploited in a high-control group?

_____
_____
_____
_____
_____
_____
_____
_____
_____
_____
_____
_____
_____
_____
_____
_____
_____
_____
_____
_____
_____

"Books can be dangerous. The best ones should be labeled 'This could change your life.'" — Helen Exley

Alternative Healing Modalities
(The Challenge to Heal, page 235)

Have you used any of these alternative therapies (or others) to help with your recovery from control abuse? How has that worked?

"When in doubt, walk out!" Marcelo Santos III

What is next for you?

"The modern world has called us to a maturity we are not capable of if all we have is blind faith and literalism."
Thomas Keating

What is your vision for your life now?

"All life has emptiness at its core; it is the quiet hollow reed through which the wind of God blows and makes the music that is our life." Wayne Muller

Have you developed specific goals that will help you realize your vision? Outline them here.

"However vast the darkness, we must supply our own light."   Stanley Kubrick

Have you developed concrete steps to reach those goals? (You can outline the steps you intend to take on a few different goals on the next few pages.)

"If a man does not keep pace with his companions, perhaps it is because he hears a different drummer. Let him step to the music which he hears, however measured or far away." Henry David Thoreau

Summarize what you have learned about yourself and life, due to the entire experience of being in a high-control group and getting out of a high-control group.

"The human spirit is too large to accept a cage for its home." Huston Smith

"No price is too high to pay for the privilege of owning yourself."   Rudyard Kipling

Part 2
Feelings Journal Guidelines

This feelings journal is designed after Julia Cameron's (*The Artist's Way*) "Morning Pages". Cameron recommends that artists write for 30 minutes each morning when they rise, about their negative feelings so that they can approach each day free of negativity. The negative feelings are not ignored, disparaged or suppressed, but acknowledged by writing them down. The writing becomes a form of release of the feelings and frees up the body/mind to operate each day without the weight of hidden, unaddressed negativity. Survivors of high-control groups can benefit from employing this same strategy.

The use of a *Feelings Journal* for recovery from high-control group abuses is outlined in Chapter 11, "Documenting Your Story" in the book *The Challenge to Heal*. The book describes the process as follows:

"**How to adapt Cameron's morning pages idea to your high-control group exit experience:** If you find yourself experiencing a lot of grief and pain or harboring a lot of bitterness and resentment about your life in the group, **create a second journal dedicated solely to expressing your feelings**. Use this second "morning pages" journal to allow the full and free expression of the negative feelings for **thirty minutes every morning**. You may have to rise a little earlier than usual to allow time for this. (Writing about your negative thoughts and painful feelings at the end of the day is less desirable. It can interfere with a peaceful night's sleep and adversely affect your dreams.)

The procedure is, that once you have released the resentments and hurts in your journal, you then promise yourself not to fall back into those feelings again that day. Just that day**.** The next morning will dawn and you grant yourself another thirty minutes of unbridled expression in your **dedicated feelings journal** ... By so doing, you are acknowledging the feelings, honoring their existence, then placing them in a secure place so that you don't have to carry them around in your body/mind all day. This is a healthy, every-day form of releasing the burden of justified negativity.

Recording morning pages a la Julia Cameron helps you accept and honor the feelings that are still lurking in you, but limits their expression to a certain time and place every day. This frees you up for the rest of the day to enjoy and explore life, to be creative and productive without interference from heavy, negative states about years of servitude and coercion in the group. This is a powerful act of self-care and self-empowerment.

If during the day negative thoughts about your high-control group experience sneak in anyway, simply stop them, and say "Not now". Then 'remind them' you will give them an opportunity for expression the next morning. Cameron's "morning pages" will then have been adapted by you as a sort of limited, daily, personal debriefing – a releasing of any pain, sadness, resentment, anger, bitterness onto the welcoming, non-judgmental screen or page.

In this free-form, "morning pages" journaling project, do not concern yourself with appearance or style. Just write. There are no extra points for perfect prose or artistic design. For thirty minutes of journaling about your feelings - anything goes. One proviso however, is that you should stop if you see yourself becoming too emotional or worked up. The important thing is to **keep it all in proportion, safe, contained in the journal***, and limited to thirty minutes. Deal? Deal!"* (Excerpted from The Challenge to Heal, pages 57-58.) Be sure to date and cross-reference (if needed) everything in this workbook and journal.

Feelings Journal, Date: _____

_____
_____
_____
_____
_____
_____
_____
_____
_____
_____
_____
_____
_____
_____
_____
_____
_____
_____
_____
_____
_____
_____
_____
_____
_____

"A personal journal is an ideal environment in which to "become". It is a perfect place for you to think, feel, discover, expand, remember, and dream." Brad Wilcox

Feelings Journal, Date: _____

"Fill your paper with the breathings of your heart." William Wordsworth

Feelings Journal, Date: _____

"Those who insist they've got their 'shit together' are usually standing in it at the time." *Stephen Levine*

Feelings Journal, Date: _____

"You have to quit confusing a madness with a mission." Flannery O'Connor

Feelings Journal, Date: _____

"I would rather have a mind opened by wonder than one closed by belief." Gerry Spence

Feelings Journal, Date: _____

"Until you realize how easy it is for your mind to be manipulated, you remain the puppet of someone else's game."
Evita Ochel

Feelings Journal, Date: _____

"If we climb high enough, we will reach a height from which tragedy ceases to look tragic." Irvin D. Yalom

Feelings Journal, Date: _____

"What a comfort is this journal. I tell myself to myself and throw the burden on my book and feel relieved.
Anne Lister

Feelings Journal, Date: _____

Feelings Journal, Date: _____

"Abuse doesn't define you." C. Kennedy

Feelings Journal, Date: _____

"There is something wonderfully bold and liberating about saying yes to our entire imperfect and messy life."
Tara Brach

Feelings Journal, Date: _____

"You can't manipulate people who know how to think for themselves." Trish Mercer

Feelings Journal, Date: _____

"Someone I loved once gave me a box full of darkness. It took me years to understand that this too, was a gift." Mary Oliver

Feelings Journal, Date: _____

"From the beginning men used God to justify the unjustifiable."   Salman Rushdie

Feelings Journal, Date: _____

"There are a thousand thoughts lying within a man that he does not know till he takes up the pen to write."
William Makepeace Thackeray

Feelings Journal, Date: _____

"Nobody knows what God's plan is for your life, but a whole lot of people will guess for you if you let them."
Shannon L. Adler

Feelings Journal, Date: _____

"...we may often mistake the record of what we have been for a prescription of what we can become." Frances Vaughan

Feelings Journal, Date: _____

"Beware of those who try to sell you simple answers to complex questions." Scott Adams

Feelings Journal, Date: _____

"Meaning makes things endurable, perhaps everything." Carl Jung

Feelings Journal, Date: _____

"It is the certainty that they possess the truth that makes men cruel."   Anatole France

Feelings Journal, Date: _____

"I now see how owning our story and loving ourselves through that process is the bravest thing that we will ever do."
Brené Brown

Feelings Journal, Date: _____

"Fundamentalism isn't about religion, it's about power." Salman Rushdie

Feelings Journal, Date: _____

"When you feel caught in the web of childhood abuse, find words to describe it. Write them. Say them. Express them. In safe places, with safe people." *Jeanne McElvaney*

Feelings Journal, Date: _____

"From fanaticism to barbarism is only one step." Denis Diderot

Feelings Journal, Date: _____

"Every situation, properly perceived, becomes an opportunity to heal." *A Course in Miracles*

Feelings Journal, Date: _____

"Indoctrination is premeditated murder of the mind." Andrea L'Artiste

Feelings Journal, Date: _____

"Freedom is the capacity to pause between stimulus and response." Rollo May

Feelings Journal, Date: _____

"Do not be so open-minded that your brains fall out." G.K. Chesterton

Feelings Journal, Date: _____

"Every sunset is an opportunity to reset." Richie Norton

Feelings Journal, Date: _____

"Those who are capable of tyranny are capable of perjury to sustain it." — Lysander Spooner

Feelings Journal, Date: _____

"There is comfort in knowing that you don't have to pretend anymore, that you are going to do everything within your power to heal." Ellen Bass

Feelings Journal, Date: _____

"Just because something isn't a lie does not mean that it isn't deceptive. A liar knows that he is a liar, but one who speaks mere portions of truth in order to deceive is a craftsman of destruction." Criss Jami

Feelings Journal, Date: _____

"I want to unfold. I do not want to remain folded up anywhere, because wherever I am still folded, I am untrue."
Rainer Maria Rilke

Feelings Journal, Date: _____

"Depression is the inability to construct a future." Rollo May

Feelings Journal, Date: _____

"Life is not a matter of holding good cards, but of playing a poor hand well." Robert Louis Stevenson

Feelings Journal, Date: _____

"Life demands for its fulfillment and completion a balance of joy and sorrow."   Carl Jung

Feelings Journal, Date: _____

"The best revenge is to be unlike him who performed the injury."   Marcus Aurelius

Feelings Journal, Date: _____

"Teach us to delight in simple things." Rudyard Kipling

Feelings Journal, Date: _____

"This is your life. You are responsible for it. You will not live forever. Don't wait." — Natalie Goldberg

Feelings Journal, Date: _____

"No matter how great you pretend to be, it is not as great as you truly are." Haven Trevino

Feelings Journal, Date: _____

"Open yourself to discomfort. Meet it with mercy, not fear." Stephen Levine

Feelings Journal, Date: _____

"Find a place where there's joy, and the joy will burn out the pain."   Joseph Campbell

Feelings Journal, Date: _____

"Fortify yourself with contentment for this is an impregnable fortress." Epictetus

Feelings Journal, Date: _____

(In a few days you will come to the end of the space allotted for your *Feelings Journal* in this workbook. To continue this important work of journaling challenging feelings, purchase yourself a book for this purpose. That way, there will be no gap in your journal entries.)

Feelings Journal, Date: _____

"To be fully alive is to feel that everything is possible." Eric Hoffer

Feelings Journal, Date: _____

"Life has no meaning. Each of us has meaning and we bring it to life. It is a waste to be asking the question when you are the answer." Joseph Campbell

Feelings Journal, Date: _____

"My accident really taught me just one thing: the only way to go on is to go on. To say 'I can do this' even when you know you can't." Stephen King

Feelings Journal, Date: _____

"History, despite its wrenching pain, cannot be unlived, and if faced with courage, need not be lived again." —Maya Angelou

Feelings Journal, Date: _____

"The secret of change is to focus all of your energy, not on fighting the old, but on building the new."   Socrates

Feelings Journal, Date: _____

"It's important to live life with the experience, and therefore the knowledge, of its mystery and of your own mystery. This gives life a new radiance, a new harmony, a new splendor." — Joseph Campbell

Feelings Journal, Date: _____

"The happiness of your life depends upon the quality of your thoughts." — Marcus Aurelius

Feelings Journal, Date: _____

"Instructions for living a life: Pay attention. Be astonished. Tell about it." *Mary Oliver*

This is the last page of your morning *Feelings Journal*. It is now time to continue this expression of feelings work in another book you purchase and dedicate to this endeavor. You can, however, continue to document your story and your healing process in the workbook Part 1 section of this book. It is my deepest hope that this companion volume to *The Challenge to Heal* has facilitated your unique process of recovering from any high-control situation, undue influence, exploitation and/or abuse.

Bonnie Zieman
Montreal, Canada
October 11, 2016

Part 3

Extra Pages

*E*xtra Pages to expand on any of the above topics, especially those from Part 1 – Documenting Your Story section of this book. (Be sure to cross-reference page numbers of the same topic.)

Further notes continuing from page _____.

_____
_____
_____
_____
_____
_____
_____
_____
_____
_____
_____
_____
_____
_____
_____
_____
_____
_____
_____
_____
_____
_____
_____

Further notes continuing from page _____.

Further notes continuing from page _____.

Further notes continuing from page _____.

Further notes continuing from page _____.

Further notes continuing from page _____.

Further notes continuing from page _____.

Further notes continuing from page _____.

Further notes continuing from page _____.

Further notes continuing from page _____.

Further notes continuing from page _____.

Further notes continuing from page _____.

Further notes continuing from page _____.

Further notes continuing from page _____.

Further notes continuing from page _____.

Further notes continuing from page _____.

Further notes continuing from page _____.

Further notes continuing from page _____.

Further notes continuing from page _____.

Further notes continuing from page _____.

Further notes continuing from page _____.

Further notes continuing from page _____.

"If you own this story, you get to write the ending." Brené Brown

Made in the USA
Columbia, SC
13 September 2017